Developing Conscious Negotiation: Elevate Your Game with Specialized Training, Navigate Patterns, and Unleash Proven Hacks in the Art of Negotiation

BY:

Kyle S. Blair

Kyle S. Blair 2024

About the Author

Meet Kyle S. Blair, the master of negotiation! Imagine a person who has dealt with high-stakes situations and has been in the trenches of deal-making. This isn't your ordinary creator; it is a person who has developed a strategy for success based on real-world negotiation experiences.

Our creator isn't about elevated hypotheses; when faced with difficult choices, they all focus on the nitty-gritty, the things that work.
This author has the inside scoop on how to make negotiations not only smooth but also downright masterful, whether they are dealing with everyday situations, personal relationships, or business.

So, buckle up and get ready to take a ride with an author who not only loves to tell stories but also gives advice that only comes from real-world negotiations. Prepare to enter the world of our extraordinary negotiation storyteller!
Kyle S. Blair 2024

❖

Contents

Reviews

Hey,

Hope you're doing awesome! ✹ Just wanted to drop you a quick note to say THANK YOU for checking out [Book Title]. I hope it brought a bit of negotiation magic to your reading world.

Now, I've got a favor to ask – could you share your thoughts on the book? Your review could be the nudge someone needs to jump into the world of negotiation wizardry. Whether it's on Amazon, Goodreads, or wherever you usually shout about awesome reads, your words matter. Ready to spill the tea? Here's the link: [Link to Book on Platform]. Hit it up whenever you've got a moment.

And, hey, feel free to dish out what you loved or any lightbulb moments you had. Your take on the book is like a secret sauce that makes our reading community even cooler.

Thanks a bunch for being part of the reading adventure!

Cheers,

[Kyle]

CHAPTER ONE

INTRODUCTION TO NEGOTIATION

Negotiating is just part of being human, you know? It's woven into everything—from how we navigate our personal relationships to sealing the deal in business or even smoothing things over on the global stage. It's like the secret sauce that flavors our everyday interactions.

Having a real heart-to-heart chat? It requires more than just talking. You've got to really tune in, show some understanding, get a bit creative, and be ready to tackle the tricky stuff. It's like the topmost skill set for deep, meaningful conversations.

It is a unique cycle where people or gatherings take part in conversations to determine clashes, simply decide, or essentially impact others. Discussion can take different forms, like distributive exchange, where gatherings contend to guarantee the most worth, or integrative discussion, where the emphasis is on making esteem and extending the general pie for the two players.

Key components of viable exchange incorporate comprehension the interests and inspirations of all gatherings included, recognizing shared view, and investigating savvy fixes that address the issues of everybody. Asides, social mindfulness and the ability to appreciate people on a deeper level assume urgent parts in exploring the intricacies of talks in different and multicultural settings.

In proficient settings, exchange abilities are exceptionally esteemed and can essentially affect a person's or alternately association's prosperity. Excelling at exchange prompts ideal results as well as encourages better connections and understanding between parties, preparing for cooperative and commonly valuable organizations. As exchange keeps on molding the manner in which people and organizations collaborate, understanding its standards and methods is fundamental for anybody looking to succeed in different parts of life.

1. Grasping the Craft of Discussion

Exchange is often portrayed as workmanship since it includes a mix of key reasoning, relational abilities, and imagination. Excelling at discussion goes beyond observing a bunch of inflexible guidelines; it requires a profound comprehension of human brain research, powerful correspondence, and the capacity to adjust to various circumstances. Here are key angles that add to figuring out the specialty of discussion:

- ❖ **Preparation**: Fruitful moderators focus on exploring the topic, figuring out the other party's point of view, and expecting potential results. Careful planning

❖

structures the underpinning of viable talks, empowering one to introduce undeniable claims and answer capably during conversations.

* **Undivided attention**: A central expertise in discussion is the capacity to listen effectively. Negotiators are able to establish compatibility, adjust their emotions, and get to a worthwhile agreement by taking into account the concerns, sentiments, and fundamental interests of the opposing side. Undivided attention shows regard and cultivates a helpful climate.

The ability to understand people on a deeper level: Feelings frequently run high during exchanges. Monitoring one's own feelings is urgent, and it is urgent to perceive close-to-home prompts from others. Sincerely clever mediators can deal with their sentiments, relate to the feelings of others, and explore tense circumstances with artfulness.

❖ **Relational abilities**: Clear and brief correspondence is essential. Moderators should explain their focuses successfully, guaranteeing that their message is perceived by all gatherings included. This includes verbal correspondence as well as non-verbal signals like non-verbal communication and looks.

❖ **Adaptability:** The capacity to adjust to changing conditions and switch procedures when important is a sign of talented moderators. Adjusting to changes allows arbitrators to check various choices, defeat stalemates, and track down imaginative answers for issues.

❖ **Building Connections**: Exchange isn't just about the ongoing arrangement; it's tied in with building long-haul connections. It is necessary to keep up with trust and validity. Fruitful mediators center around making commonly valuable arrangements that fulfill both prompt requirements and future yearnings.

❖ **Tolerance and Constancy**: Talks can be tedious and may require numerous rounds of conversations. Persistence is imperative to enduring difficulties and it is reached by persevering until a great understanding.

❖

2. Psychology of Negotiation: What Drives Human Behavior

Negotiation is a psychological dance between individuals or parties with distinct desires and motivations. Understanding the psychological aspects of negotiation is paramount for achieving successful outcomes. Here's a glimpse into what drives human behavior in the context of negotiation:

- **Needs and Desires**: At the heart of negotiation are human needs and desires. People negotiate to satisfy essential needs such as security, recognition, and belonging. Recognizing these fundamental needs in oneself and others provides insight into the underlying motivations guiding negotiation strategies.

Perception of being fair The perception of being fair significantly influences human behavior in negotiations. Individuals tend to be more cooperative when they believe the process and outcome are fair. Being biased can lead to resentment and conflict, undermining the negotiation process.

- **Risk Aversion**: Humans are generally risk-averse, preferring known outcomes over uncertain ones. Grasping this believe system helps negotiators develop proposals in ways that minimize perceived risks, making agreements more enticing.
- **Loss Aversion**: People tend to strongly prefer avoiding losses over acquiring equivalent gains. This acts a major role in negotiation. Skilled negotiators frame offers to emphasize what the other party stands to lose by not agreeing, making the deal more attractive.
- **Anchoring**: The first offer in a negotiation often serves as an anchor point, influencing the entire negotiation process. Parties tend to adjust their offers and counteroffers based on this initial reference point. Savvy negotiators strategically set anchors to their

advantage, shaping the subsequent discussions.

- **Cognitive Biases**: Various cognitive biases, such as confirmation bias (favoring information that confirms preexisting beliefs) and availability heuristic (overvaluing readily available information), impact decision-making during negotiations. Being aware of these unfair, enables negotiators to counteract their effects and make more rational choices.

- **Emotions:** Feelings assume a critical part in discussion. Dread, outrage, and energy can impact the exchange interaction and results. Sincerely shrewd mediators can perceive and deal with their own feelings while understanding the feelings of others, taking into account more powerful correspondence and affinity building.

- **Social Impact**: Social elements, including normal practices, notoriety, and friend pressure, can impact exchange results.

Individuals frequently change their conduct in light of cultural assumptions and the assessments of others. Talented mediators influence social impact elements to influence sentiments and choices in support of themselves.

- **Power Elements**: Power differences between gatherings can significantly affect exchanges. Whether it's master power (information and skill), coercive power (capacity to rebuff), or referent power (charm and amiability), understanding power elements assists moderators with exploring the discussion cycle and equilibrium the battleground.

Recognizing the mental underpinnings of exchange is vital to dominating this unpredictable craftsmanship and accomplishing results that fulfill the interests all gatherings included.

3.Fostering a Discussion Outlook: Certainty and Planning

Exchange is however much a psychological distraction as it seems to be an essential one. Fostering an exchange outlook established in certainty and exhaustive readiness essentially upgrades the possibilities accomplishing good results. This is the way certainty and readiness converge in the realm of discussion:

(A) Confidence

- **Faith in Self**: Trust in discussion begins with self-conviction. At the point when mediators genuinely trust their capacities, they are bound to declare their positions actually, draw in proactively, and handle testing circumstances with **balance.**
- **Positive Attitude**: A positive mentality can be a strong resource. Certainty breeds hopefulness, flexibility, and the capacity to see misfortunes as any open doors to learn and change methodologies. Positive

moderators are more open to effective fixes and are better at keeping up with compatibility, even in troublesome conversations.

+ **Dealing with Feelings:** Certainty empowers arbitrators to deal with their feelings, remain formed under tension, and answer mindfully to different situations. Genuinely steady arbitrators can explore intense discussions without turning out to be excessively responsive or disturbed.

(B) Preparation

+ **Information is Power**: Careful readiness is the foundation of fruitful exchange. Figuring out the topic, the interests, everything being equal, and potential impediments permits mediators to go with informed choices.

- **Expecting Situations**: Viable readiness includes expecting potential situations and arranging reactions. By taking into account various results and contriving procedures for every, moderators can adjust quickly during conversations.

- **Building Believability**: Good to go arbitrators show believability. At the point when moderators show a profound comprehension of the subject and come ready with raw numbers, they construct entrust with the other party. Believability improves the influence of their contentions and recommendations.

- **Defining Clear Objectives**: Planning assists in setting with clearing, sensible objectives for the discussion. Forms the ideal results, understand the needs, and lay out benchmarks for progress. Lucidity of objectives gives guidance and concentration during the exchange interaction.

+ **Pretending and Practices**: Participating in pretending activities and practices with associates or coaches can recreate genuine exchange situations. This training allows arbitrators to refine their correspondence, try various ideas and get counter ideas, developing their general readiness. Basic Discussion capacities

+ **Examination and Data Social affair**: Completely research the topic and the other party. Information is power in discussion.

+ **Self-awareness**: Grasp your feelings, triggers, and predispositions. Mindfulness assists you with dealing with your feelings successfully.

+ **Empathy:** Come at the situation from the other party's perspective to grasp their feelings and viewpoints.

Compassion   fabricates compatibility and trust

CHAPTER TWO

Essential Negotiation Skill Active Listening: The Key to Understanding Your Counterpart

Negotiation is a complex and nuanced process that requests a scope of abilities to be executed really. Dominating these fundamental exchange abilities can significantly upgrade your capacity to explore different circumstances and secure positive results. Here are some key exchange abilities:

(a) Relational abilities

- **Undivided attention**: The capacity to listen effectively and sympathetically to comprehend the other party's point of view is vital. Listening permits, you to reveal fundamental interests and concerns.

- **Lucidity and Brevity**: Impart your thoughts plainly and briefly. Vagueness can prompt misconceptions, so being expressive is indispensable.
- **Non-Verbal Correspondence**: Non-verbal communication, looks, and motions can convey so a lot, while possibly not more, than words. Monitoring your own non-verbal prompts and understanding others' signs improves correspondence.

(b) Critical thinking and Innovativeness:

- **Insightful Reasoning**: Examine complex circumstances, distinguish examples, and pursue information driven choices.
- **Creativity**: Investigate inventive arrangements and consider some fresh possibilities. Inventive critical thinking can prompt commonly valuable arrangements.

(c) Emphaticness and Certainty:

❖

- ✚ **Self-assured Correspondence**: Obviously express your necessities, interests, and limits. Self-assuredness shows that you esteem your viewpoint while regarding others.
- ✚ **Confidence**: Have faith in your capacities and the benefits of your contentions. Certainty improves your believability and enticement. Independent direction:
- ✚ **Risk Appraisal**: Assess possible dangers and vulnerabilities related with various results. Understanding dangers illuminates your choices.
- ✚ **Ideal Direction**: Go with choices immediately when fundamental. Delaying can prompt botched open doors or horrible results.

(d) Discussion Morals:

- ➢ **Integrity**: Maintain moral principles and tell the truth in your communications. Trust is the groundwork of fruitful talks.

Kyle S. Blair 2024

❖

➤ **Fairness:** Make progress toward fair and impartial arrangements that consider the interests of all gatherings included.

(e) Adaptability:

❖ **Flexibility:** Be available to changing conditions and change your methodologies likewise. Unbending nature can prompt stalemates.

(f) Tolerance and Determination:

❖ **Patience**: Talks frequently take time. Persistence permits you to sit tight for the right second and keep away from incautious choices.
Persistence: Continue on despite difficulties. Diligence can break gridlocks and lead to leap forwards.

(g) Post-Discussion Assessment:

▪ **Learning Direction**: Consider past exchanges to recognize what functioned admirably and what could be gotten to the

❖

next level. Consistent acquiring improves your abilities after some time.

By improving these fundamental exchange abilities, you can move toward dealings with certainty, explore intricacies, and encourage useful connections, prompting commonly helpful arrangements.

Methodologies and Strategies

With regards to Negotiation, methodologies and strategies are particular methodologies utilized by gatherings to accomplish their objectives and impact the result of the discussion interaction. Here is a breakdown of their implications:

1. Strategies:

Definition: Exchange methodologies are general, long haul plans or approaches utilized to accomplish explicit targets in a discussion. These are the wide techniques or structures that guide the general heading of the discussion interaction.

Instances of Systems:

- ❖ **Cooperative Procedure:** Centers around finding commonly valuable arrangements, underlining participation and relationship building.
- ❖ **Serious Procedure**: Includes seeking after one's own advantages forcefully, frequently to the detriment of the other party's inclinations.
- ❖ **Compromising Methodology**: Includes going with concessions to agree, tracking down a center ground between gatherings' positions.
- ❖ **Aversion Methodology**: Includes deferring or staying away from the exchange cycle out and out, frequently utilized while the timing isn't positive or when issues can be settled through different means.

Kyle S. Blair 2024

❖

❖ **Obliging Procedure**: Includes focusing on the other party's inclinations over one's own, frequently used to save connections or when issues are not of high significance.

2. Tactics:

Definition: Discussion strategies are explicit activities or methods utilized inside the exchange cycle to acquire a benefit, impact the other party, or steer the discussion toward an ideal result. Strategies are the quick, transient moves utilized during exchanges.

❖ **Instances of Strategies**:
❖ **Opening with a High or Low Anchor**: Setting the underlying proposal at an outrageous worth to impact the scope of satisfactory results.
❖ **Silence:** Utilizing quietness decisively to urge the other party to make concessions or uncover more data.
❖ **Nibbling:** Setting little extra demands or expectations after the primary

❖

understanding is reached to acquire additional worth.

- ❖ **Great Cop, Terrible Cop**: One party embraces a helpful, well-disposed approach (great cop), while another party takes a harder, fiercer position (terrible cop) to make close to home strain.
- ❖ **Leave:** Taking steps to end the discussion and leave, expecting to initiate the other party to make better concessions.
- ❖ **Building Alliances**: Framing partnerships with different gatherings engaged with the exchange to acquire strength and impact aggregate choices.

In rundown, exchange methodologies are the all-encompassing plans that guide the general methodology, while discussion strategies are the particular procedures and activities utilized inside the exchange cycle to accomplish vital goals. Fruitful mediators frequently consolidate viable methodologies with suitable strategies to explore the intricacies of dealings and accomplish great results.

Kyle S. Blair 2024

❖

CHAPTER THREE

Shared benefit Exchange: Making an incentive for The two players

Shared benefit exchange is a cooperative methodology where all gatherings included cooperate to accomplish commonly useful results. Not at all like cutthroat or ill-disposed approaches, mutual benefit exchange centers around making an incentive for everybody instead of one party "winning" to the detriment of the other. This strategy is established in the conviction that the two players can accomplish their objectives without compromising the other's situation. This is the way mutual benefit discussion makes an incentive for all gatherings included:

1. Figuring out Interests:

❖ **Recognizing Needs**: In mutually advantageous discussion, parties dig into one another's inclinations and necessities.

❖

Understanding these hidden worries permits arbitrators to track down intelligent fixes that address the interests of the two sides.

- ❖ **Shared Objectives**: Finding normal goals assists in building arrangements that with satisfying shared interests, making an establishment for a commonly fulfilling result. Open Correspondence:
- ❖ **Transparency**: Transparent correspondence is fundamental. Parties share applicable data, concerns, and limitations, encouraging trust between them.
- ❖ **Undivided attention**: Each party listens effectively to the next point of view, exhibiting appreciation and understanding. Listening helps in recognizing regions where concessions or compromises can be made without forfeiting fundamental interests.

❖

2. Innovative Critical thinking:

- **Brainstorming**: Parties participate in imaginative meetings to generate new ideas to investigate different choices. This energizes inventive reasoning and the disclosure of arrangements that may not be evident at first.
- **Extending the Pie**: Shared benefit exchange intends to grow the allegorical pie, importance making more worth than recently envisioned. This can include investigating extra assets, taking into account various factors, or including different partners to improve the likely results.

3.Adaptability and Flexibility:

- **Adaptation**: Parties stay adaptable and open to changing their positions in light of new data or evolving conditions. Being versatile permits mediators to really answer surprising difficulties.

Kyle S. Blair 2024

- **Trade-offs**: Mutual benefit discussions frequently include compromises, where gatherings make concessions in certain areas to acquire benefits in others. This readiness to think twice about cooperation.

4.Long haul Connections:

- **Relationship Building:** Mutual benefit discussion underscores the significance of building long haul connections. Positive, cooperative encounters in exchanges can prompt future organizations and coordinated efforts.
- **Trust and Regard**: By esteeming each other's necessities and exhibiting regard, parties lay out trust, which is indispensable for feasible connections.

5. Understanding Toughness:

- **Strong Arrangements**: Since shared benefit exchange tends to the fundamental interests of the two players, the subsequent arrangements will generally be more vigorous and persevering. They are less inclined to prompt struggles or debates from here on out

The ability to understand people at their core:

Close to home Guideline: Parties deal with their feelings actually, keeping gloomy feelings from wrecking the discussion interaction. The capacity to understand people on a profound level aide in keeping a positive air helpful for cooperation.

+ **Empathy:** Understanding the feelings and points of view of the other party encourages sympathy, permitting mediators to find arrangements that oblige each other's feelings.

Basically, mutual benefit exchange is tied in with encouraging a helpful, critical thinking mentality where the two players effectively add to finding arrangements that expand an incentive for all interested parties. By zeroing in on understanding interests, open correspondence, imaginative critical thinking, adaptability, relationship building, and the ability to appreciate anyone on a deeper level, shared benefit exchange makes maintainable arrangements that leave all gatherings fulfilled and happy with the result

Serious Strategies: When and How to Utilize Them

Serious strategies in exchange include a more emphatic and vital methodology where one party expects to get the most ideal result for themselves, frequently to the detriment of the other party. While these strategies can be viable in specific circumstances, they ought to be utilized wisely and morally. This is when and the way to involve cutthroat strategies in discussion:

When to Utilize Cut Throat Strategies:

❖ **At the point when There is Restricted Data**: Cutthroat strategies can be utilized when one party has essential data that the other party needs. This data deviation can be utilized to acquire a benefit.

❖

- ❖ **In Profoundly Aggressive Business sectors:** In businesses with extreme contest, organizations frequently utilize serious strategies to get more ideal arrangements. It becomes fundamental to be confident to keep an upper hand.
- ❖ **While Safeguarding Primary concerns**: Assuming safeguarding your main concern or monetary soundness is vital, cutthroat strategies can be utilized to arrange good terms that guarantee productivity and manageability.
- ❖ **In One-time or Momentary Exchanges**: Cutthroat strategies may be suitable in circumstances where gatherings don't anticipate participating in ongoing dealings or keep up with long haul connections.
- ❖ **While Confronting Untrustworthy or Forceful Partners**: Assuming that the other party is utilizing forceful strategies, it very well may be important to utilize cutthroat methodologies with good reason to forestall being exploited.

❖

Step by step instructions to Utilize Serious Strategies:

➤ **Set High Desires**: Begin with aggressive objectives. Setting high desires gives you space to make concessions while as yet accomplishing a palatable result.

➤ **Uncover Data Specifically**: Uncover data decisively. Uncovering just what is important can keep the other party dubious and keep them from expecting your best courses of action.

➤ **Make a Need to get a move on:** Presenting cutoff times or underlining the earnestness of the circumstance can pressure the other party into settling on quicker choices, possibly in support of yourself.

➤ **Use Quiet as a Strategy:** Quiet can be a useful asset. Subsequent to making a deal, stay quiet. The other party could feel a sense of urgency to fill the quietness by making concessions.

➢ **Utilize Jump Responses**: Respond firmly (or appear to) to recommendations. Express amazement or disillusionment to cause the other party to reexamine their situation, conceivably prompting better terms for you.

➢ **Make Gradual Concessions**: On the off chance that you really want to make concessions, do so steadily. Little concessions give the presence of give and take without altogether influencing your situation.

➢ **Take steps to Leave**: In the event that the exchange isn't going in support of yourself, be ready to take steps to leave. This strategy can in some cases take the other party back to the table with further developed offers.

➢ **Utilize Cutthroat Offering**: In obtainment or business contracts, cutthroat offering cycles can be utilized to guarantee the most ideal terms from providers or project workers.

Moral Contemplations:

- ✓ **Stay away from Double dealing**: While utilizing serious strategies, it is vital to stay legit. Stay away from misdirection, as it can hurt your standing and harm connections over the long haul.
- ✓ **Regard Limits**: Cutthroat strategies shouldn't cross moral or legitimate limits. Stay away from strategies that are manipulative, coercive, or unlawful.
- ✓ **Keep up with Impressive skill**: Indeed, even in serious talks, keep an expert disposition. Forcefulness shouldn't convert into discourteousness or aggression.

Serious strategies can be successful when utilized nicely and in the right setting.

Kyle S. Blair 2024

❖

Nonetheless, arbitrators ought to continuously gauge the transient additions against likely long haul results, and utilize these strategies wisely and morally to accomplish the most ideal results for all gatherings included.

Cooperative Methodologies: Fabricating Long Haul Connections

Cooperative methodologies in discussion center around building long haul connections and commonly helpful results. These techniques underline participation, open correspondence, and critical thinking. Utilizing cooperative techniques helps in agreeing as well as cultivates trust and understanding between parties. This is the way to fabricate long haul connections involving cooperative methodologies in exchange:

1. Open Correspondence:
✓ **Transparency**: Be transparent about your inclinations, concerns, and imperatives. Straightforward correspondence lays out

❖

trust and makes way for a cooperative environment.

✓ **Undivided attention**: Give close consideration to the next party's point of view. Listening effectively shows regard and assists you with grasping their requirements better.

✓ **Joint Critical thinking**:

✓ **Brainstorming:** Empower imaginative meetings to generate new ideas where the two players can produce different thoughts. This cooperative methodology frequently prompts creative arrangements.

✓ **Recognizing Shared belief**: Look for shared belief and shared interests. Stress the regions where your objectives adjust to construct an establishment for collaboration.

2. Center around Interests, Not Positions:

✓ **Interest-Based Exchange**: Rather than unbendingly adhering to positions, investigate the fundamental interests of the two players. Seeing each other's necessities takes into account more adaptable and effective fixe.

- ✓ **Pose Unassuming Inquiries**: Urge the other party to talk about their inclinations and concerns. Genuine inquiries welcome point by point reactions, giving significant bits of knowledge.

3. Building Trust and Validity:

- ✓ **Reliability**: Be dependable and steady in your activities and commitments. Unwavering quality forms trust in your capacity to satisfy responsibilities.

- ✓ **Shared Values**: Accentuate shared values and shared objectives. Adjusting your exchange approach with shared standards encourages a feeling of solidarity.

4. Cooperative Direction:

- ✓ **Agreement Building**: Make progress toward agreement where the two players are really happy with the understanding. Cooperative direction guarantees that the arrangement addresses the issues of all included.

Kyle S. Blair 2024

✓ **Integrate Criticism**: Be available to criticism and reexamine proposition in view of the other party's feedback. This adaptability shows your obligation to cooperation.

5. Long haul Point of view:

✓ **Center around Relationship Building**: View exchanges as a chance to construct a drawn out relationship. Focus on the relationship over quick gains, understanding that trust and collaboration yield benefits over the long run.

✓ **Consistent Commitment**: Remain drew in with the other party even after the exchange closes. Customary correspondence helps in keeping up with the relationship and tending to any worries that might emerge.

6. Compromise:

✓ **Address Clashes Valuably:** Clashes are a characteristic piece of any relationship. Address them transparently and usefully, zeroing in on finding arrangements that fulfill the two players' necessities.

✓ **Intercession and Help**: In the event that clashes heighten, consider including a nonpartisan outsider to work with correspondence and guide the goal cycle.

7. **Underscore Shared Benefit Results**:

✓ **Shared Advantages**: Take a stab at results where the two players benefit. Shared benefit arrangements upgrade the readiness to team up from now on and fortify the relationship.

✓ **Fairness**: Guarantee that the appropriation of advantages is seen as fair by all gatherings. Seen reasonableness supports trust and altruism.

By embracing cooperative methodologies, moderators can accomplish prompt arrangements as well as lay out getting through connections in view of trust, regard, and shared targets. These connections give a strong groundwork to future joint efforts and organizations, adding to long haul accomplishment for all gatherings included

❖

Managing Troublesome Characters: Exploring Testing Discussion Circumstances

Managing troublesome characters in discussion requires a blend of tolerance, the capacity to understand people on a profound level, and vital correspondence. Troublesome characters can appear in different ways, like animosity, resignation, control, or tenacity. Here are techniques for exploring testing discussion circumstances:

1. **Keep even headed and Made:**
✓ **Profound Guideline**: Hold your feelings under wraps. Answer smoothly regardless of whether the other party becomes angry. Close to home control exhibits your

impressive skill and can de-heighten tense circumstances.

✓ **Enjoy Reprieves if necessary**: On the off chance that the discussion turns out to be excessively warmed, recommend enjoying some time off to chill. This break can give the two players an opportunity to recover and move toward the conversation with a new point of view.

2. **Active Listening and Empathy:**

✓ **Listen Actively**: Pay close attention to the difficult person's concerns and emotions. Active listening demonstrates that you value their perspective, which can help diffuse hostility.

✓ **Show Empathy**: Try to understand their viewpoint and acknowledge their feelings. Demonstrating empathy can create a sense of validation and may lead to a more cooperative attitude.

3. **Set Boundaries**:

✓ **Be Firm**: While being empathetic, maintain assertiveness. Clearly communicate your boundaries and what behavior is unacceptable. Setting firm, respectful boundaries helps establish a professional tone for the negotiation.

- ✓ **Avoid Escalation**: Refrain from responding to hostility with more hostility. Instead, calmly assert your boundaries without engaging in personal attacks.

4. **Build Rapport:**

- ✓ **Find Common Ground**: Look for shared interests or experiences. Building rapport, even on a small scale, can create a sense of connection that can positively influence the negotiation atmosphere.

- ✓ **Use Positive Reinforcement**: Acknowledge and appreciate any positive behavior or cooperation displayed by the difficult person. Positive reinforcement can encourage more favorable behavior.

5. **Stay Solution-Focused:**

- ✓ **Redirect the Focus**: Steer the conversation back to the issues at hand and the solutions being discussed. Avoid getting sidetracked by personal attacks or irrelevant topics.

✓ **Frame Solutions Positively**: Emphasize the benefits of the proposed solutions to the difficult person. Positive framing can make them more receptive to the ideas being presented.

6. Collaborative Problem-Solving:

✓ **Involve Them**: Engage the difficult person in problem-solving. Involving them in the process can give them a sense of control and may reduce resistance.

✓ **Seek Their Input**: Ask for their opinions and suggestions. Demonstrating that their input is valued can encourage cooperation.

7. Consider Mediation:

✓ **Neutral Third Party**: If the situation doesn't improve, consider involving a mediator. A neutral mediator can facilitate communication and guide the negotiation toward a more productive direction.

8. Document Agreements:

- ✓ **Clarity and Accountability**: Clearly document any agreements reached. Having a written record ensures clarity and holds all parties accountable, reducing the likelihood of disputes later on.

9. **Know When to Walk Away**:

- ✓ **Recognize Deal-Breakers**: If the difficult person's behavior is consistently obstructive and negotiations are unproductive, be prepared to consider walking away.

Dealing with difficult personalities in negotiation requires a combination of assertiveness, empathy, and effective communication. By staying composed, setting boundaries, building rapport, and focusing on solutions, negotiators can navigate challenging situations and work towards reaching mutually beneficial agreements.

❖

CHAPTER FOUR

Advanced Negotiation Techniques

Advanced negotiation techniques go beyond the basics, requiring a deep understanding of human psychology, communication, and strategic thinking. Here are some advanced techniques to enhance your negotiation skills:

a. BATNA and ZOPA:

- **BATNA** (Best Alternative to a Negotiated Agreement): Always be aware of your BATNA, which is your best alternative if the current negotiation fails. Knowing your BATNA gives you leverage.

❖

- **ZOPA** (Zone of Possible Agreement): Identify the range in which an agreement is possible. Skilled negotiators expand the ZOPA through creative solutions, ensuring both parties benefit.

b. Emotional Framing:

- **Emotional Appeal**: Appeal to the other party's emotions, needs, and desires. Understanding their emotional drivers can influence their decisions significantly.

- **Emotional Contagion**: Display positive emotions to create a positive atmosphere. Emotions are contagious and can affect the mood of the negotiation.

c. Cognitive Biases:

- **Exploit Cognitive Biases**: Understand common cognitive biases such as anchoring, confirmation bias, and framing effect. Use this knowledge to influence the other party's decisions.

- **Mitigate Your Own Biases**: Be aware of your own biases and work to mitigate their influence on your decisions. Objectivity is crucial in negotiations.

d. Strategic Use of Silence:

- **Tactical Silence**: Strategic pauses can prompt the other party to fill the silence, potentially revealing more information or making concessions.
- **Active Listening in Silence**: Use silence to actively listen and process the other party's statements. Silence can also show that you are considering their points seriously.

e. Logrolling:

- **Mutual Concessions**: Identify issues where your preferences differ and make concessions on items that matter less to you but are significant to the other party. This fosters goodwill and encourages reciprocation.

f. Power Dynamics:

- **Expert Power:** Demonstrate expertise and knowledge in the subject matter. Expertise can enhance your credibility and influence.

- **Referent Power**: Build rapport and establish a likable People are more likely to agree with individuals they like and respect.

g. Negotiation Jujitsu:

- **Deflecting and Reframing**: Instead of directly opposing an argument, deflect it and reframe it to your advantage. This technique involves redirecting negative or aggressive statements.

- **Agreeing without Agreement**: Agree with the other party's perspective without conceding your position entirely. This acknowledges their viewpoint without compromising your stance.

h. Analytical Techniques:

- **Decision Trees**: Use decision trees to evaluate different possible outcomes and their probabilities. This analytical approach helps in making strategic decisions.

- **Game Theory**: Understand the basics of game theory to anticipate the other party's moves and formulate responses based on their likely strategies.

i. **Cross-Cultural Negotiation**:

- **Cultural Sensitivity**: Be aware of cultural differences in negotiation styles, communication norms, and decision-making processes. Adjust your approach to accommodate diverse cultural perspectives. Persistent Learning:

- **Post-Exchange Examination**: Think about finished exchanges to dissect what worked and what didn't. Gain from the two victories and disappointments to refine your methodologies.

- **Role-Playing**: Take part in pretending activities to reproduce different exchange situations. Practice improves your versatility and thinking abilities.

High level discussion procedures require a nuanced comprehension of human way of behaving, successful correspondence, and an essential outlook. By integrating these procedures and constantly improving your abilities, you can explore complex dealings effectively and accomplish ideal results

Owner Elements in Discussion: Perceiving and Utilizing Wellsprings of Force

1. Social Contemplations in Worldwide Exchanges

Social contemplations assume a crucial part in worldwide dealings. Understanding and regarding social contrasts can altogether influence the progress of global agreements and joint efforts. Here are key viewpoints to consider while taking part in worldwide discussions:

2. Social Mindfulness and Responsiveness:
   ✓ **Research Societies**: Concentrate on the social standards, customs, and

correspondence styles of the nations you are managing. Understanding social subtleties assists you with exploring discussions all the more really.

✓ **Abstain from Generalizing**: Societies are different, and people inside a culture can shift broadly. Keep away from speculations and treat every individual as a person.

3. **Correspondence Styles:**

✓ **Direct versus Circuitous Correspondence**: A few societies favor direct correspondence, while others utilize backhanded language to pass on messages. Understanding this distinction forestalls mistaken assumptions.

✓ **High-Setting versus Low-Setting Societies**: High-setting societies depend on setting, non-verbal signs, and connections for correspondence. In low-setting societies, correspondence is express and depends less on setting.

4. **Relationship Building:**

- ✓ **Building Trust**: In many societies, trust is significant before business discussions can advance. Concentrate profoundly on building connections, sharing feasts, and participating in friendly exercises to lay out trust.
- ✓ **Convention and Regard**: Regard for ordered progression and convention differs across societies. Tending to people with proper titles and showing regard for position can improve your believability.

5. Dynamic Styles:

Agreement versus Individual Independent direction: A few societies favor arriving at choices through agreement, including various partners. Others depend on individual chiefs. Comprehend the dynamic cycle in the way of life you are managing.

6. Time Direction:

Monochromic versus Polychromic Societies: Monochromic societies center around each assignment in turn and worth dependability.

Kyle S. Blair 2024

❖

Polychromic societies handle numerous undertakings all the while and have a more loosened up perspective on time. Adjust your methodology as needs be.

7. **Discussion Styles:**
   - ✓ **Serious versus Helpful Societies**: A few societies have a more cutthroat exchange style, while others lean toward a helpful methodology. Understanding the social inclination can direct your exchange procedure.
   - ✓ **Face-Saving**: Many societies esteem face-saving and keeping away from public shame. Be prudent in resolving issues to safeguard nobility.

8. **Gift-Giving and Decorum**:
   - ✓ **Gift-Giving Traditions**: Comprehend the suitable events for giving gifts and the sorts of gifts that are socially OK. In certain societies, gift-giving is a huge part of relationship building.
   - ✓ **Eating Manners**: Eating customs can differ broadly. Look into legitimate eating

manners to keep away from unexpected blunder.

9. **Dealing with Conflicts and Clashes**:
   - ✓ **Aberrant Articulation of Conflict**: In certain societies, conflict might be communicated in a roundabout way to keep up with concordance. Focus on non-verbal signals and unpretentious clues.
   - ✓ **Outsider Intervention**: In specific societies, including an impartial outsider may be the favored technique to determine clashes. Be available to intervention assuming that the circumstance warrants it.

10 **Lawful and Moral Contemplations**:
   - ✓ **Lawful Contrasts**: Find out more about the legitimate structures in the country you are haggling with. Regulations connected with contracts, protected innovation, and strategic policies can shift fundamentally.
   - ✓ **Social Awareness in Consistence**: Comprehend and regard social standards while guaranteeing your strategic

approaches line up with global lawful and moral guidelines.

11 Constant Learning and Versatility:

- ✓ **Input and Variation**: Look for criticism from neighborhood accomplices or social experts. Adjust your methodology in light of the criticism got.
- ✓ **Gains from Errors**: In the event that misconceptions happen, break down them, gain from the experience, and change your systems for future dealings.

In worldwide dealings, social capability is an important resource. Monitoring social contrasts, adjusting your correspondence style, and recognizing assorted traditions and standards can encourage positive connections and lead to effective and commonly helpful results in worldwide transactions

Moral Exchange: Genuinely trustworthy offsetting Desire

Moral exchange includes directing talks with genuineness, trustworthiness, and reasonableness. It underscores building connections, safeguarding trust, and making commonly gainful results without undermining one's ethical standards. Offsetting desire with uprightness in discussion is fundamental for keeping up with believability, encouraging long haul connections, and guaranteeing the supportability of arrangements. Here are key standards to think about in moral discussion:

Kyle S. Blair 2024

1. **Straightforwardness and Trustworthiness**:

- **Truthfulness**: Be honest about your aims, capacities, and constraints. Stay away from embellishments, bogus commitments, or misdirecting articulations.
- **Disclosure**: Reveal pertinent data regardless of whether it could put you in a tough spot.

Moral arbitrators focus on transparency over essential covering.

2. **Regard and Pride:**

- **Aware Correspondence**: Approach all gatherings with deference, no matter what their situation or foundation. Utilize considerate language and keep an expert tone.
- **Nobility in Conflict**: Handle conflicts with nobility and amazing skill. Stay away from individual assaults or belittling

language in any event, when contrasts become obvious.

3. Decency and Value:

- **Fair Offers**: Make fair and sensible offers. Moral mediators try not to take advantage of the other party's weaknesses or making exorbitantly uneven proposition.

- **Equivalent Treatment**: Treat all gatherings engaged with balance and decency. Try not to show partiality or segregation in view of individual predispositions.

4. Honesty and Consistency:

- **Consistency**: Maintain reliable standards and norms across talks. Keep away from twofold guidelines or changing positions in view of the discussion's specific situation.

- **Commitments and Responsibilities**: Satisfy commitments and responsibilities made during dealings. Your honesty is essential for building trust.

❖

5. Compassion and Understanding:

- **Empathy**: Figure out the other party's point of view and feelings. Compassionate mediators are bound to track down arrangements that meet the veritable requirements of all gatherings included.

- **Social Awareness**: Be socially touchy and aware of social contrasts. Social comprehension forestalls false impressions and exhibits regard for variety.

6. Long haul Connections:

- **Center around Relationship Building**: Moral mediators focus on the drawn out relationship over prompt increases. Feasible connections are based on trust; which moral conduct sustains.

- **Compromise**: Address clashes productively and morally. Look for goals that are fair and accommodating of every one of gatherings' inclinations.

7. Social Obligation:

❖

- **Natural and Social Effect**: Think about the more extensive effect of your discussions on the climate and society. Moral discussion incorporates careful thought of social and natural obligations.
- **Corporate Social Obligation**: On the off chance that appropriate, adjust discussion systems to corporate social obligation drives. Moral practices improve an organization's standing.

8. **Nonstop Reflection and Improvement**:

- **Self-Reflection**: Consistently ponder your discussion rehearses. Survey whether your techniques line up with moral standards and make changes depending on the situation.
- **Gaining from Moral Quandaries**: Dissect past dealings, particularly those including moral situation Gain from these encounters to upgrade your moral independent direction.

9. **Moral Administration**:

- **Setting Moral Models**: Pioneers in talks ought to set moral models for their groups. Showing moral way of behaving supports moral practices inside the association.
- **Preparing and Training**: Give preparing and training on moral exchange rehearses inside your association. Furnish moderators with the abilities to morally explore complex circumstances.

Offsetting desire with respectability in discussion requires serious areas of strength for a compass, sympathy, and a promise to decency. Moral arbitrators focus on long haul connections, genuineness, and social obligation, guaranteeing that their activities line up with moral standards and contribute emphatically to the more extensive local area. By maintaining moral principles, mediators can accomplish aggressive objectives while keeping up with their trustworthiness and the admiration of their partner

Haggling in High-Stakes Circumstances: Emergency The board and Direction

Kyle S. Blair 2024

Haggling in high-stakes circumstances, particularly during emergencies, requires an extraordinary arrangement of abilities, versatility, and a quiet, essential methodology. Here are techniques for powerful emergency the board and dynamic in high-stakes exchanges.

1) **Remain cool-headed and Centered**:
- **Profound Control**: Stay totally under control, even in high-pressure circumstances. Close to home steadiness takes into account unwavering discernment and objective navigation.
- **Center around Goals**: Obviously characterize your goals and needs. Center around the main thing, and try not to get occupied by minor issues or feelings.

2) **Careful Readiness**:
- **Situation Arranging**: Expect different emergency situations and plan your reactions. Having alternate courses of action considers fast transformation to evolving conditions.

❖

- **Risk Appraisal**: Evaluate possible dangers and vulnerabilities related with various results. Figure out the expected results of every choice.

3) **Compelling Correspondence**:

- **Clear and Direct Correspondence**: Be clear, brief, and direct in your correspondence. Vagueness can prompt errors, which are particularly hindering in emergency circumstances.

- **Undivided attention**: Listen effectively to the worries and points of view of all gatherings included. Understanding their positions can give important bits of knowledge to tracking down arrangements.

4) **Dynamic Methodologies**:

- **Fast Independent direction**: High-stakes circumstances frequently require brief choices. Survey the accessible data, assess the dangers, and settle on choices expeditiously when vital.

- **Informed Choices**: Accumulate however much applicable data as could reasonably be expected prior to simply deciding. Informed choices are bound to be successful and dependable.

5) **Building Partnerships**:

- **Alliance Building**: Structure unions with partners who share normal interests. Building an alliance can reinforce your situation and increment your impact during dealings.

- **Group Coordinated effort**: Work together intimately with your group and influence their mastery. A bound together group improves direction and emergency the board capacities.

6) **Keep up with Adaptability**:

- **Adaptability**: High-stakes circumstances can change quickly. Be ready to adjust your techniques and reactions in light of developing conditions.

- **Elective Arrangements**: Investigate various arrangements and think about unpredictable methodologies. Imaginative critical thinking can prompt leap forwards in emergency discussions.

7) **Moral Contemplations**:

- **Integrity**: Maintain moral norms even in high-stress circumstances. Moral way of behaving reinforces your validity and cultivates trust, which is fundamental for emergency the board.

- **Fairness**: Take a stab at fair and impartial arrangements, taking into account the interests of all gatherings included. Reasonableness improves the acknowledgment of arrangements.

8) **Discussion Power Elements**:

- **Survey Power Elements**: Comprehend the power elements among the gatherings in question. Evaluating power connections helps in creating key methodologies.

- **Use Power Shrewdly**: Assuming that you have power advantage, use it prudently.

❖

Pressure or abuse of force can prompt disdain and upset long haul connections.

9) **Post-Emergency Assessment**:

- Learning Direction: After the emergency is settled, lead an intensive assessment. Recognize what functioned admirably and what could be gotten to the next level. Gaining from the experience upgrades your emergency the executive's abilities for what's in store.

10) **Connect with Impartial Middle people:**

- **Mediation**: In exceptionally touchy and quarrelsome circumstances, consider including a nonpartisan outsider as a go between. A gifted middle person can work with correspondence and guide the discussion towards goal.

Haggling in high-stakes circumstances requires a blend of key preparation, compelling correspondence, flexibility, and moral navigation. By keeping composed under tension, teaming up with the right partners, settling on educated and convenient choices, and gaining from every emergency circumstance, arbitrators can actually explore even the most difficult conditions and secure great results

CHAPTER FIVE

Key Illustration: Correspondence and Tact

1. The Cuban missile crisis (1962)

Key example: Communication and Diplomacy

Action item: During this emergency, open channels of correspondence between pioneers (Kennedy and Khrushchev) helped de-heighten pressures. Discretionary endeavors, alongside backchannel discussions, assumed a critical part in forestalling an atomic struggle.

2. Camp David Accords (1978):

Key Example: Determination and Tolerance

Action item: President Jimmy Carter's patient and determined strategy brought Egyptian President Anwar Sadat and Israeli State leader Menachem Start together. The discussions

Kyle S. Blair 2024

prompted a noteworthy truce among Egypt and Israel, displaying the force of steadiness in complex dealings.

3. Arrival of American Prisoners from Iran (1981):

Key Example: Building Connections

Focus point: In the background dealings between the U.S. furthermore, Iran, interceded by Algeria, in the long run prompted the arrival of American prisoners. Building trust and encouraging associations with mediators assumed a vital part in the dealings.

4. Nelson Mandela and the Finish of Politically-sanctioned racial segregation (1994):

Key Illustration: Absolution and Compromise

Focal point: Mandela's ability to pardon his oppressors and work towards compromise set up for tranquil talks. Embracing absolution and zeroing in on the future, as opposed to the past, can make ready for effective compromise.

5. Iran Atomic Arrangement (2015):

Key Illustration: Comprehensive Exchange and Tact

Focal point: Comprehensive exchanges including different nations (P5+1) and worldwide associations prompted the Iran Atomic Arrangement. Drawing in different partners and making an extensive understanding addressing the worries of all gatherings added to the outcome of the discussion.

6. **US-China Stage One Economic alliance (2020):**

Key Example: Adaptability and Split the difference

Focus point: The two players made compromises to arrive at a fractional economic agreement, facilitating pressures in the continuous exchange war. Adaptability and an eagerness to think twice about specific issues can prompt break arrangements, encouraging a steadier arranging climate.

7. . **Israel-UAE Nonaggression treaty (2020):**

Key Example: Intercession and Spanning Partitions

Important point: The nonaggression treaty among Israel and the UAE was worked with by the US. Intercession and connecting the split between countries with authentic contentions can prompt earth shattering arrangements, even in well-established questions.

8. . Coronavirus Immunization Supply Talks (2021):

Key Example: Cooperative Critical thinking

Focus point: Worldwide endeavors to arrange Coronavirus antibody supply arrangements required cooperation between states, drug organizations, and global associations. Cooperative critical thinking and a common need to get going can drive talks even in high-stakes, time-delicate circumstances.

Normal Important points:

Effective Communication: Open and honest communication is crucial in negotiations, fostering understanding and trust between parties.

Relationship Building: Building strong relationships with stakeholders, intermediaries, and opposing parties can facilitate smoother negotiations.

Flexibility and Adaptability: Being willing to adapt strategies and make concessions can lead to mutually beneficial agreements.

Mediation and Third-Party Involvement: Neutral third parties can facilitate discussions and bridge gaps between parties with entrenched positions.

Breaking down Discussion Disappointments: Understanding Slip-ups and How to Stay away from Them

Examining exchange disappointments is vital for individual and expert development. Understanding the missteps made and gaining from them can assist moderators with keeping away from comparative traps from here on out.

Here are normal exchange disappointments, the examples to be gained from them, and methodologies to stay away from these slip-ups:

1. **Absence of Arrangement**:

Failure: Insufficient examination and absence of arrangement debilitate your situation and breaking point your exchange procedures.

Lesson: Completely research the subject, grasp the partner's point of view, and expect likely difficulties.

How to avoid it: Focus on research, distinguish your objectives, and plan for potential situations and counterarguments.

2. **Unfortunate Correspondence**:

Failure: Miscommunication, hazy messages, or false impressions can prompt breakdowns in talks.

Lesson: Be clear, brief, and unambiguous in your correspondence. Listen effectively to grasp the other party's point of view.

How to avoid it: Practice undivided attention, utilize clear language, and look for criticism to guarantee common comprehension.

3. Disregarding The ability to appreciate anyone at their core:

Failure: Overlooking or misusing feelings can prompt aggression, harmed connections, and block viable correspondence.

Lesson: Foster capacity to appreciate individuals on a deeper level to grasp your feelings and those of others. Deal with feelings, particularly during high-stakes talks.

How to avoid it: Practice sympathy, control your feelings, and know about non-verbal prompts to precisely measure the close to home environment.

4. Sitting above Social Contrasts:

Kyle S. Blair 2024

❖

Failure: Disregarding or misjudging social subtleties can prompt misconceptions and offense, hurting the discussion cycle.

Lesson: Instruct yourself about social contrasts, correspondence styles, and normal practices of the gatherings in question.

How to avoid it: Move toward talks with social responsiveness. Adjust your correspondence style and conduct to regard social variety.

5. Absence of Adaptability:

Failure: Unbending nature and a reluctance to think twice about lead to gridlock and bombed exchanges.

Lesson: Be available to elective arrangements and concessions. Adaptability is critical for settling on something worth agreeing on.

How to avoid it: Focus on your objectives yet adjust your methodology. Recognize regions where you can make concessions without compromising fundamental interests.

Kyle S. Blair 2024

❖

6. Nonattendance of Trust:

Failure: Absence of trust between gatherings can prevent open correspondence and split the difference, prompting fruitless talks.

Lesson: Construct trust by tell the truth, dependable, and reliable in your activities and words. Trust is the groundwork of effective dealings.

How to Avoid it: Exhibit uprightness, satisfy guarantees, and be straightforward to lay out and keep up with entrust with the other party.

7. Zeroing in Exclusively on Cost:

Failure: Overemphasis on cost can disregard other significant parts of the arrangement, like quality, terms, or long haul connections.

Lesson: Consider the general incentive. Arrange terms, quality, and extra advantages, in addition to the cost.

How to avoid it: Assess the whole arrangement exhaustively. Try not to limit talks down to a solitary perspective; think about the more extensive picture.

8. Heightening Contentions as opposed to Overseeing Them:

Failure: Permitting clashes to raise without addressing them valuably can prompt unfriendly conditions.

Lesson: Address clashes speedily and valuably. Try to figure out the hidden issues and work towards goal.

How to avoid it: Cultivate a positive environment. Address clashes carefully and include nonpartisan outsiders if important to intercede questions.

9. Overlooking BATNA (Best Option in contrast to an Arranged Understanding):

Failure: Not having an unmistakable comprehension of your BATNA can prompt tolerating negative arrangements.

Lesson: Continuously know your BATNA. It gives you influence and assists you with assessing the allure of the arranged arrangement.

Avoidance: Evaluate and fortify your BATNA prior to entering discussions. Having areas of strength for an enables your exchange position.

10 Absence of Post-Discussion Assessment:

Failure: Forgetting to break down the discussion results can keep gaining from botches and botched open doors.

Lesson: Assess both fruitful and ineffective dealings. Comprehend what worked, what didn't, and why.

Kyle S. Blair 2024

❖

How to avoid it: Ponder exchange results consistently. Examine victories and disappointments to recognize regions for development in ongoing exchanges. By disappointments and incorporating the illustrations learned, moderators can improve their abilities, stay away from normal entanglements, and move toward future dealings with a more educated and key mentality. Constant gaining from the two victories and disappointments is fundamental for turning into a capable and compelling.

CHAPTER SIX

Practical Applications

Negotiation skills are applicable in various aspects of life, from business and career to personal relationships. Here are some practical applications of negotiation skills:

I. **Business and Professional Settings**:

Contract Negotiations: Negotiating terms and conditions with suppliers, clients, or partners to establish mutually beneficial contracts.

Salary and Benefits: Negotiating salary, bonuses, benefits, and work conditions with employers. Sales and Marketing: Persuading customers, closing deals, and establishing partnerships with other businesses.

Partnerships and Alliances: Negotiating terms for joint ventures, collaborations, and strategic alliances to expand business opportunities.

Conflict Resolution: Mediating disputes among employees, teams, or departments within an organization.

II.   Entrepreneurship:

Funding and Investments: Negotiating funding, equity stakes, or loans with investors, venture capitalists, or banks.

Business Development: Negotiating distribution deals, licensing agreements, and contracts with suppliers or manufacturers.

III.   Real Estate:

Buying and Selling Property: Negotiating the price, terms, and conditions when buying or selling real estate.

Renting and Leasing: Negotiating lease terms, rent, and conditions for residential or commercial properties.

IV. Legal Professions:

Settlement Agreements: Negotiating settlements in legal disputes to avoid going to court.

Client Representation: Negotiating terms and conditions on behalf of clients in legal matters.

V. International Relations and Diplomacy:

Trade Agreements: Negotiating international trade agreements and treaties between countries.

Conflict Resolution: Mediating between conflicting parties in international disputes or conflicts.

VI. Personal relationships: Negotiating household's chores, responsibilities, and parenting duties in family.

Kyle S. Blair 2024

Conflict Resolution: Resolving disagreements with friends, family, or romantic partners through effective communication and compromise.

VII. **Community Engagement**:

Community Projects: Negotiating terms with local authorities or organizations for community projects and initiatives.

Advocacy and Activism: Negotiating with policymakers or organizations to advocate for social change or charitable causes.

VIII. **Consumer Situations:**

Customer Service: Negotiating refunds, replacements, or solutions with customer service representatives in case of product or service issues.

Viable Applications

Discussion abilities are pertinent in different parts of life, from business and vocation to individual connections. Here are a few reasonable utilizations of negotiation abilities:

a. Business and Expert Settings:

Contract Dealings: Arranging agreements with providers, clients, or accomplices to lay out commonly valuable agreements.

Compensation and Advantages: Arranging pay, rewards, advantages, and work conditions with managers.

Deals and Advertising: Convincing clients, shutting bargains, and laying out associations with different organizations.

Associations and Coalitions: Arranging expressions for joint endeavors, coordinated efforts, and vital partnerships to grow business amazing open doors.

Compromise: Intervening questions among workers, groups, or offices inside an association.

b. Entrepreneurship:

Financing and Ventures: Arranging subsidizing, value stakes, or advances with financial backers, investors, or banks.

Business Improvement: Arranging dispersion bargains, authorizing arrangements, and agreements with providers or producers.

c. Land:

Trading Property: Arranging the value, terms, and conditions while trading land.

Leasing and Renting: Arranging lease terms, lease, and conditions for private or business properties.

d. Lawful Callings:

Settlement Arrangements: Arranging settlements in lawful questions to try not to go to court.

Client Portrayal: Arranging agreements for the benefit of clients in lawful issues.

e. Worldwide Relations and Tact:

Economic deals: Arranging global economic deals and settlements between nations.

Compromise: Intervening between clashing gatherings in worldwide questions or clashes.

f. Individual Connections:

Family Matters: Arranging family errands, obligations, and nurturing obligations in family settings.

Compromise: Settling conflicts with companions, family, or significant others through viable correspondence and split the difference.

g. **Local area Commitment:**

Local area Undertakings: Arranging terms with nearby specialists or associations for local area ventures and drives.

Support and Activism: Haggling with policymakers or associations to advocate for social change or admirable missions.

h. **Purchaser Circumstances**:

Client support: Arranging discounts, substitutions, or arrangements with client support agents if there should be an occurrence of item or administration issues.

Vehicle acquisitions: Arranging the cost and terms while purchasing a vehicle, including exchange ins and supporting.

i. **Schooling and The scholarly world:**

Scholarly Exploration: Arranging research coordinated efforts, associations, and awards with different establishments or associations.

Kyle S. Blair 2024

❖

Understudy Undertakings: Arranging grants, monetary guide, and study courses of action with instructive foundations.

j. Medical services and Clinical Field:

Protection Cases: Arranging health care coverage cases and inclusion with protection suppliers.

Clinical Independent direction: Arranging treatment choices and choices with medical services experts for customized care plans.

Exchange abilities are flexible and appropriate in various settings. Creating successful exchange abilities can prompt improved results, further developed connections, and upgraded critical abilities to think in different parts of life.

Haggling in Business: Agreements, Associations, and Arrangements

Haggling in the business world is a basic expertise that can essentially influence the achievement and development of an organization. Whether you're chipping away at agreements, associations, or arrangements, successful discussion techniques are fundamental. Here are a few vital ways to haggle in business settings:

A. Exhaustive Readiness:

Grasp Your Necessities: Obviously characterize your targets and needs. Understand what you need to accomplish from the exchange.

Research: Accumulate data about the other party, market norms, and industry guidelines. Information is power in exchanges.

Expect Difficulties: Distinguish expected obstructions and plan reactions or elective arrangements ahead of time.

B. **Viable Correspondence:**

Undivided attention: Give close consideration to the next party's interests and points of view. Listening effectively shows regard and helps in grasping their necessities.

Clear Articulation: Convey your focuses plainly and compactly. Use language that is unambiguous and maintains a strategic distance from false impressions.

Non-verbal communication: Know about your non-verbal communication and that of the other party. Positive and certain non-verbal communication can improve your believability.

C. **Building Connections:**

❖

Lay out Trust: Trust is the groundwork of fruitful talks. Tell the truth, solid, and satisfy vows to construct entrust with the other party.

Empathy: Figure out the feelings and worries of the other party. Understanding their viewpoint can make a positive discussion climate. Discussion Systems:

BATNA: Know your Best Option in contrast to an Arranged Understanding (BATNA). It gives you influence and certainty during talks.

Anchoring: Make the principal offer if conceivable. The underlying proposition frequently fills in as an anchor, affecting the remainder of the discussion.

Shared benefit Approach: Hold back nothing arrangements where the two players feel happy with the result. Shared benefit exchanges cultivate long haul connections.

D. **Adaptability and Split the difference**:

Be Adaptable: While keeping up with your center advantages, be available to thinks twice about less basic focuses. Adaptability can prompt arrangement.

Inventive Critical thinking: Think inventively to track down arrangements that address the two players' issues. In some cases, unpredictable methodologies can prompt creative arrangements.

E. Lawful Comprehension:

Lawful Ability: Include lawful specialists to audit agreements and arrangements.

Understanding the legitimate ramifications is pivotal to stay away from future debates.

Compliance: Guarantee that the arranged terms agree with significant regulations, guidelines, and industry principles.

F. Finalizing the Negotiation:

Sum up Arrangements: Obviously frame the settled upon terms prior to finalizing the negotiation. This guarantees shared understanding.

See everything through to completion: Honor the responsibilities made during exchanges. Satisfy guarantees instantly to keep up with trust.

G. Post-Exchange Assessment:

Survey and Learn: After the discussion, direct a posthumous investigation. Survey what functioned admirably and what could be moved along. Gain from every exchange insight.

H. Social Awareness:

Figure out Social Contrasts: In the case of haggling globally, know about social subtleties and adjust your way to deal with deference social variety.

Interpret Archives: Assuming managing parties from various language foundations, guarantee that all archives are precisely meant keep away from mistaken assumptions.

I. **Compromise:**

Mediation: On the off chance that talks arrive at a stalemate, consider including an unbiased outsider or go between to work with conversations and resolve clashes.

Haggling in business requires a blend of readiness, powerful correspondence, key reasoning, and moral direct. By applying these standards and consistently refining your exchange abilities, you can explore agreements, associations, and arrangements effectively, encouraging positive and productive connections for your business.

Negotiating in Private Life: Connections, Funds, and Ordinary Circumstances

Exchange abilities are not restricted to the business world; they are fundamental in private life also. Whether it's managing connections, funds, or regular circumstances, successful discussion can prompt better figuring out, further developed connections, and commonly acceptable results. Here are a few ways to haggle in private life:

i. **Correspondence and Undivided attention:**

Express Your Necessities: Obviously well-spoken your requirements, concerns, and assumptions. Be transparent about what you need from the discussion.

significant for settling on something worth agreeing on.

ii. **Relationships:**

❖

Listen effectively: Focus on the other individual, understanding their view point and perspective is important.

Empathy: Come at the situation from the other individual's perspective. Understanding their feelings and concerns can assist you with tracking down splits the difference in clashes.

Regard Limits: Regard each other's limits and individual space. Haggling in connections includes understanding and regarding individual cutoff points.

iii.   **Finances:**

Planning and Spending: Arrange planning and ways of managing money with relatives. Track down a harmony among requirements and needs to successfully oversee funds.

Obligation and Credits: In the case of managing obligation, arrange reimbursement plans with banks. Be proactive and convey what is going on truly.

Kyle S. Blair 2024

❖

iv. **Circumstances**:

Family Tasks: Arrange family obligations and errands. Circulate assignments genuinely founded on every individual's capacities and accessibility.

Youngsters and Nurturing: In the event that pertinent, arrange nurturing liabilities, rules, and discipline techniques with your accomplice.

Social Commitments: Impart your solace levels with respect to get-togethers, social occasions, and family capabilities. Arrange plans that suit the two accomplices.

v. **Compromise**:

Keep even headed: Try to avoid panicking during clashes. Profound guideline is critical to settling issues usefully.

Use "I" Articulations: Express your sentiments and concerns utilizing "I" articulations to try not to sound accusatory. For instance, say, "I feel upset when..." rather than "You always..."

Kyle S. Blair 2024

❖

Center around Arrangements: Shift the concentration from accusing to tracking down arrangements. Conceptualize together to distinguish ways of resolving the issue.

vi. Significant Choices:

Compromise: Think twice about significant choices, like moving, evolving position, or major monetary speculations. Find arrangements that oblige the two accomplices' goals and necessities.

Long haul Arranging: Haggle long haul plans, like retirement investment funds, lodging, and vocation ways. Adjust your objectives and work together towards normal targets.

vii. Apologize and Pardon:

Apologize Earnestly: Assuming that you're off base, apologize truly. Recognize your missteps and focus on setting things right.

Forgiveness: Be available to excusing others. Clutching feelings of resentment obstructs useful discussion and goal.

viii.   **Taking care of oneself and Limits**:

Put down Stopping points: Obviously characterize your own limits and convey them to other people. Regard others' limits too.

Taking care of oneself Discussion: Arrange time for taking care of oneself and individual pursuits inside the setting of connections and family obligations.

ix.   **Look for Proficient Assistance**:

Counseling: In the event that private matters endure, think about looking for the assistance of a specialist or guide. Proficient arbiters can work with useful conversations and deal direction.

x.   **Ceaseless Correspondence**:

Normal Registrations: Have standard registration discussions with your accomplice or relatives. Open correspondence encourages understanding and resolves likely issues before they raise.

Haggling in private life requires sympathy, persistence, and a readiness to track down splits the difference. By encouraging open correspondence, figuring out others' points of view, and being deferential of limits, you can explore connections, funds, and regular circumstances with elegance and common regard. Recollect that discussion in private human existence amounts to much more than winning or losing yet about tracking down arrangements that work for all interested parties.

Negotiation in the Computerized Age: Online Stages and Virtual Correspondence

Ordinary Registrations: Have normal registration discussions with your accomplice or relatives.

Open correspondence cultivates understanding and resolves likely issues before they raise. Haggling in private life requires sympathy, persistence, and an eagerness to track down splits the difference. By cultivating, open correspondence, figuring out others' view points and being conscious of limits. You can explore connections, funds, and regular circumstances with elegance and common regard winning or losing however about tracking down arrangements that work for all interested parties.

Discussion in the Advanced Age: Online Stages and Virtual Correspondence

Discussion in the computerized age has gone through huge changes because of the approach of online stages and virtual specialized devices. With the ascent of the web and different advanced stages, talks can now happen across borders, bringing new open doors and difficulties. Here are methodologies for compelling discussion in the advanced age:

❖ **Pick the Right Stage**:

Select Proper Instruments: Utilize dependable and secure internet based stages for discussions. Email, Video Conferencing, and devoted

❖

discussion stages offers various elements, Pick the one that suits your requirements.

Information Security: Focus on stages with strong safety efforts to safeguard delicate data during discussions.

❖ **Lay out Clear Correspondence**:

Set Clear Assumptions: Obviously frame the discussion interaction, cutoff times, and assumptions.

Lay out guidelines for virtual discussions.

Settle on Correspondence Channels: Decide the essential correspondence channel (email, video calls, informing applications) and guarantee all gatherings are open to utilizing it.

❖ **Develop an Expert Internet based Presence**:

Proficient Profiles: Keep up with proficient profiles via web-based entertainment and expert systems administration destinations. Your internet based presence can impact how you are seen during dealings.

Email Manners: Utilize proficient language and organizing in messages. Be compact and clear in

your correspondence to stay away from errors.

❖ **Successful Virtual Correspondence**:

Dynamic Commitment: Remain connected with during virtual gatherings. Utilize verbal prompts, motions, and gesturing to show mindfulness.

Obvious Signals: Use video calls whenever the situation allows. Looks and non-verbal communication convey significant signals in exchanges.

Kyle S. Blair 2024

❖

❖ **Plan Computerized Documentation**:

Computerized Arrangements: Plan very much organized advanced archives. Use PDF designs for arrangements, recommendations, and agreements. Electronic marks can smooth out the endorsement interaction.

Variant Control: Obviously name record renditions and updates to stay away from disarray about the most recent changes.

❖ Improve Specialized Capability:

Specialized Commonality: Dive more deeply into different advanced instruments and their highlights. A fundamental comprehension of virtual correspondence innovations is fundamental.

Specialized Help: Approach specialized help in the event of network issues during significant talks.

- ❖ **Beating Social Hindrances**:

Social Responsiveness: Know about social contrasts, particularly in virtual worldwide talks. Adjust your correspondence style to be conscious of assorted social standards.

- ❖ **Embrace Computerized Joint Effort Devices**:

Cooperative Stages: Utilize cooperative instruments like Google Work area, Microsoft Groups, or Slack for constant record altering and texting.

Project The executives: Execute project the board apparatuses to monitor exchange progress, errands, and cutoff times.

- ❖ **Information Protection and Security:**

❖

Encryption: Utilize scrambled correspondence channels to safeguard delicate information. Guarantee that the stages you use conform to information security guidelines.

Classification Arrangements: Consider consenting to advanced classification arrangements when essential, particularly while sharing delicate data.

❖ **Post-Exchange Follow-Up**:

Affirmation Messages: Send itemized follow-up messages summing up central issues and arrangements came to during virtual exchanges. This aide in keeping away from mistaken assumptions.

Booked Audits: Plan occasional virtual gatherings to survey progress, address concerns, and guarantee that the two players are satisfying their responsibilities.

In the computerized age, effective talks require versatility, specialized capability, and a sharp

❖

comprehension of virtual correspondence subtleties. By utilizing fitting devices, keeping up with impressive skill, and being aware of computerized behavior, moderators can tackle the capability of online stages to encourage compelling and useful discussions in a globalized world.

CONCLUSION AND FUTURE OF NEGOTIATION

THE FUTURE OF NEGOTITAION

The future of negotiation is being determined by various budding trends and technologies, changes the way people engages in discussions, make deals and resolve conflicts. Here are the key areas driving the future of negotiation:

- ❖ **Artificial Intelligence (AI) and Machine Learning**:

Automated Negotiation: AI-driven algorithms can analyze vast amounts of data, predict trends, and suggest optimal negotiation strategies.

Chat bots and Virtual Negotiation Assistants: AI-powered chat bots can assist in preliminary negotiations, answering queries, and providing real-time data.

❖ **Block chain Technology:**

Smart Contracts: Block chain enables the creation of smart contracts, which are self-executing contracts with terms directly written into code. These contracts automatically execute when conditions are met, ensuring transparency and security.

conditions are met, ensuring transparency and security.

Immutable record keeping: Block chain provides a secure, tamper-proof ledger for recording. Negotiation outcomes, agreements, and transactions.

❖ **Augmented and Virtual Reality (AR/VR):**

Virtual Negotiation Spaces: AR/VR technologies can create virtual environments where negotiators from different locations can meet, interact, and negotiate as if they were in

❖

the same room. Interactive Product Demonstrations: AR/VR can be used to showcase products or prototypes during negotiations, enhancing the understanding of offerings.

- ❖ **Data analytics and predictive modelling**
  Behavioral Analytics: Analyzing behavioral patterns and decision making processes can provide, insights into the preferences and tendencies of negotiation counterparts.

  Predictive Modelling: Predictive analytics can forecast negotiation outcomes based on historical data, enabling negotiators to make informed decisions.
- ❖ **Collaborative Platforms and Online Marketplaces**:
  Global Collaboration: outline platforms facilities collaboration among geographically dispersed teams and negotiation counterparts, enabling real-time discussions and document sharing.

Kyle S. Blair 2024

❖

Marketplace Negotiations: Digital marketplaces allow businesses to negotiate terms, prices, and conditions online, streamlining procurement processes.

❖ **Emotional AI and Sentiment Analysis**:

Emotion Recognition: Emotional AI can analyze facial expressions, tone of voice, and body language to gauge the emotional states of negotiators, aiding in understanding unspoken cues.

Sentiment Analysis: Analyzing written and verbal communication for sentiment can provide insights into the emotional tone of negotiations, enabling negotiators to respond appropriately.

❖ **Environmental and Sustainable Negotiations:**

Green Negotiations: Negotiations focusing on environmental concerns, renewable energy projects, and sustainable practices are becoming increasingly prevalent.

Kyle S. Blair 2024

❖

Carbon Trading and Emission Reduction: Negotiations related to carbon credits, emission reduction targets, and climate change mitigation strategies are gaining importance.

❖ **Personalized Negotiation Strategies:**

Individualized Negotiation Plans: AI-driven systems can analyze the negotiation style, preferences, and behavioral patterns of individuals, allowing for tailored negotiation strategies.

Adaptive Learning: Systems can learn from past negotiations and adapt strategies based on what has been successful in similar situations.

❖ **Ethical and Social Considerations**:

Ethical AI Use: Discussions surrounding the ethical use of AI in negotiations, addressing biases, transparency, and accountability.

Social Impact: Considering the social and cultural implications of negotiation outcomes, ensuring fairness and inclusivity.

❖ **Remote and Decentralized Negotiations**:

Global Remote Teams: As remote work becomes more common, negotiations involving teams from different time zones and cultures require new strategies for effective communication and collaboration.

Decentralized Decision-Making: Decentralized organizations and block chain-based governance models may influence negotiation dynamics, requiring adaptation to new power structure.

Mastering the Craft of Exchange: Proceeding with Your Learning Process

Excelling at discussion is a continuous cycle that includes consistent learning, practice, and refinement of abilities. Whether you are a fledgling or an accomplished moderator, there are multiple ways of proceeding with your learning process and upgrade your discussion skill:

❖ **High level Preparation and Studios:**

Proficient Advancement Courses: Sign up for exchange courses presented by legitimate establishments or online stages. Search for courses that covers progressed discussion methods and true contextual investigations.

Studios and Courses: Go to studios and workshops directed by discussion specialists. These occasions give potential chances to active work on, systems administration, and gaining from genuine models.

❖ **Peruse Generally**:

Books: Peruse books composed by famous exchange specialists.

Research Papers: Remain refreshed on scholarly examination in the field.

❖ **Online Assets:**

Online Gatherings: Partake in web-based gatherings and conversation bunches connected with discussion. Drawing in with a local area of moderators permits you to share encounters, look for exhortation, and gain from others.

Online classes and Web recordings: Go to online classes and pay attention to digital broadcasts facilitated by discussion experts. These stages frequently include conversations on contemporary discussion difficulties and arrangements.

❖ **Pretending and Reproduction Activities**:

Practice Meetings: Take part in pretending practices with companions or tutors. Reenact different exchange situations to improve your abilities and get productive input.

Exchange Games: Play exchange games and reproductions accessible on the web. These intuitive devices assist you with rehearsing exchange methodologies in a gamble free climate.

❖ **Mentorship and Training:**

Track down a Coach: Look for mentorship from experienced moderators. Gaining from their down to earth encounters can give significant experiences and direction.

Proficient Instructing: Consider recruiting a discussion mentor who can survey your abilities, give customized input, and assist you with

❖

creating progressed strategies. Nonstop Self-Appraisal:

Input Sales: Effectively look for criticism from discussion partners, associates, or guides. Helpful analysis can feature regions for development.

Self-Reflection: Routinely consider your exchange encounters. Dissect what functioned admirably and what should be possible in an unexpected way. Distinguish examples and regions that require consideration.

❖ **True Application:**

Apply Learning: Search for chances to apply your discussion abilities, all things considered, circumstances. Practice discussion procedures in your working environment, local area, or individual connections.

Gain from Disappointments: Embrace disappointments as opportunities for growth. Investigate fruitless discussions to grasp the

❖

basic reasons and distinguish regions for development.

❖ Develop The ability to appreciate anyone at their core:

The ability to understand people on a deeper level Preparation: Improve your capacity to appreciate people at their core abilities. The ability to appreciate people at their core is essential in grasping feelings, overseeing clashes, and building compatibility during talks.

❖ Remain Informed about Worldwide Patterns:

Worldwide Discussion Elements: Remain informed about global discussion patterns, social contemplations, and international variables. Worldwide experiences are critical for exploring complex global discussions.

Kyle S. Blair 2024

❖

- ❖ **Practice Compassion and Undivided attention:**

Compassionate Correspondence: Practice sympathy to grasp the feelings and points of view of others. Sympathy encourages trust and fortifies connections in exchanges.

Undivided attention Studios: Go to studios or instructional courses explicitly centered around undivided attention abilities. Compelling listening is central to fruitful discussion results.

Keep in mind, dominance in discussion is an excursion as opposed to an objective. By persistently looking for information, gaining from encounters, and applying new strategies, you can refine your exchange abilities and become an exceptionally capable moderator. Remain inquisitive, stay open to new methodologies, and explore constantly the craft of exchange.

Kyle S. Blair 2024

❖

Exchange Agendas and Formats

Surely! Discussion agendas and layouts can be important devices to guarantee that you cover all fundamental angles during the exchange cycle. Here are a few key components that you can remember for exchange agendas and layouts, sorted for various phases of the discussion cycle Planning Stage:

Characterize Goals: Obviously frame your objectives and what you need to accomplish from the discussion. Be explicit about wanted results.

Research: Assemble data about the other party, their inclinations, assets, shortcomings, and any significant industry guidelines.

BATNA (Best Option in contrast to an Arranged Understanding): Assess your BATNA to comprehend your backup position assuming the exchange fizzles.

Group Arrangement: In the event that haggling collectively, allot jobs and obligations to colleagues. Guarantee everybody is in total agreement with respect to discussion objectives.

❖ **During Discussion**:

Undivided attention: Effectively pay attention to the next party's assertions, concerns, and offers. Take notes if vital.

Explain and Affirm: Explain any questionable assertions or terms. Sum up and affirm arrangements occasionally to keep away from mistaken assumptions.

Flexibility: Be available to savvy fixes and elective offers. Change your methodology in view of the conversation.

❖ **Documentation and Arrangement:**

❖

Drafting the Understanding: Obviously frame the terms, conditions, obligations, and commitments of the two players in the exchange arrangement.

Legitimate Survey: Have the understanding investigated by legitimate specialists to guarantee consistence with regulations and guidelines.

Signatures: Guarantee all important gatherings consent to the last arrangement. Think about electronic marks for computerized arrangements.

❖ **Post-Discussion Follow-Up:**

Implementation: Guarantee that the two players stick to the provisions of the arrangement. Set up systems to screen progress and execution.

Review: Lead a post-exchange survey meeting with your group to evaluate what functioned admirably and regions for development.

Feedback: Look for criticism from the other party on the exchange interaction. Useful input can illuminate your future dealings.

❖ General Tips for Discussion:

Keep mentally collected: Stay cool headed even in testing circumstances. Feelings can cloud judgment and hinder powerful correspondence.

Non-verbal communication: Be aware of your non-verbal communication and notice the other party's non-verbal signals. Positive non-verbal communication can encourage trust.

Using time effectively: Deal with your time actually during exchanges. Stay away from superfluous deferrals and keep the conversation zeroed in on central issues.

Test Discussion Agenda Format:

Exchange Title:

Date:

Readiness Stage:

Characterize exchange targets.

Draft the concurrence with clear terms, conditions, and obligations.

Have the understanding audited by lawful specialists.

Guarantee all essential gatherings consent to the arrangement.

Post-Discussion Follow-Up:

Execute the particulars of the arrangement and screen progress.

Lead a post-exchange survey meeting with your group.

Look for criticism from the other party on the exchange cycle.

Kyle S. Blair 2024

General Tips:

Keep a cool head and remain mentally collected.

Be aware of non-verbal communication and non-verbal signs.

Oversee time successfully during discussions.

Utilizing a layout like this guarantees that you cover all urgent parts of the exchange cycle, advancing an organized and coordinated way to deal with your discussions. Make sure to tweak the agenda and format as per the particular setting and necessities of every discussion you attempt

❖ **Suggested Perusing and Assets**

Here is an organized rundown of prescribed understanding materials and online assets to upgrade your insight and abilities in discussion:

Books:

Kyle S. Blair 2024

❖

"**Getting to Yes**: Arranging Understanding Without Yielding" by Roger Fisher, William Ury, and Bruce Patton - An exemplary on principled exchange procedures.

"Never Put down some a reasonable compromise: Haggling, come hell or high water" by Chris Voss - Composed by a previous FBI mediator, this book offers pragmatic exchange systems and strategies.

"Anticipating Benefit: Exchange Systems for Sensible Individuals" by G. Richard Shell Gives a complete manual for exchange hypothesis and practice.

"Influence: The Brain research of Influence" by Robert B. Cialdini - Investigates the brain research behind impact and influence, significant for talks.

"The Craft of Discussion: The most effective method to Ad Lib Understanding in a Tumultuous World" by Michael Wheeler -

Offers experiences into exchange ad lib and imagination. Online Courses and Stages:

Coursera - Offers exchange courses from top colleges and organizations, including the College of California, Irvine, and the College of Michigan.

edX - Furnishes discussion courses as a team with colleges like Harvard College and Georgetown College.

LinkedIn Learning - Elements different discussion courses, including points like high level exchange strategies and multifaceted exchange.

.

Sites and Web journals: Harvard Program on Discussion (PON) - A main asset for exchange research, including articles, contextual investigations, and exchange works out.

Discussion Diary - A scholastic diary by the Worldwide Relationship for Peace making, distributing research articles on exchange hypothesis and practice.

Harvard Business Survey (HBR) - HBR's discussion area gives articles composed by specialists, offering functional counsel and experiences into exchange techniques.

Program on Exchange at Harvard Graduate School Blog - A blog offering articles, book surveys, and meetings connected with discussion and compromise.

Podcasts:

"Arrange Anything" - Facilitated by Kwame Christian, this digital broadcast covers discussion procedures and highlights interviews with exchange specialists.

"The Craft of Appeal" - Offers episodes on exchanger abilities, correspondence, and impact, highlighting master visitors.

"The Dark Swan Gathering's Exchange in all things" - Facilitated by previous FBI mediator

Chris Voss, giving commonsense discussion tips to different circumstances.

YouTube Channels:

Harvard Graduate School Program on Exchange - Elements recordings on discussion methods, talks, and conversations by eminent researchers.

Voss Exchange - Chris Voss' YouTube channel remembers recordings for discussion strategies and techniques, frequently showed with genuine models.

Make sure to investigate these assets in view of your particular advantages and objectives inside the field of exchange. Every asset offers a one of a kind point of view, permitting you to extend your comprehension and refine your exchange abilities Glossary of Discussion Terms

Absolutely! Here is a glossary of normal exchange terms to assist you with exploring the universe of talks all the more really:

A:

Kyle S. Blair 2024

BATNA (Best Option in contrast to an Arranged Understanding): The strategy a party will take on the off chance that the ongoing exchange closes in no understanding.

B:

Primary concern: The most minimal satisfactory result or proposition in an exchange.

C:

Compromise: A settlement where each side makes concessions to arrive at a commonly pleasing result.

Concession: Something given or yielded during exchange to agree.

Irreconcilable circumstance: A circumstance where an individual's confidential advantages struggle with their expert commitments in a discussion.

D:

Deadlock: A circumstance where gatherings can't agree.

Distributive Dealing: Otherwise called lose or win-lose bartering, where one party's benefit is another party's misfortune.

I:

Integrative Exchange: A helpful methodology where gatherings team up to track down a commonly useful arrangement, frequently extending the worth of the exchange.

Interests: The fundamental necessities, wants, concerns, or fears that spur a party's situation in an exchange.

L:

Leverage: The power, benefit, or impact one party has in an exchange.

Logrolling: A discussion strategy where gatherings trade favors or concessions to accomplish common increases.

Kyle S. Blair 2024

❖

M:

Mediation: A cycle where an impartial outsider assists parties in an exchange with agreeing.

Shared Gain: The standard of looking for arrangements where all gatherings benefit, known as a mutually beneficial arrangement.

N:

Nonverbal Correspondence: Correspondence without words, including non-verbal communication, looks, and signals, which can pass on significant messages in discussions.

P:

Power: The capacity to impact the way of behaving or choices of others in a discussion.

R:

Reservation Point: The most minimal satisfactory result for a moderator, otherwise called the "walkaway point." S:

❖

Settlement: A goal came to by discussion, frequently bringing about a proper understanding.

Stalemate: A circumstance where neither party in a discussion can continue or gain ground.

Meaningful Clash: A conflict about the genuine substance of issues being examined in a discussion.

Sunk Cost Deception: A mental inclination where past ventures (time, cash, exertion) lead individuals to go with choices in view of those speculations, regardless of whether the choice is at this point not judicious.

T:

One good turn deserves another: A discussion procedure where one party answers in kind to the moves of the other party, compensating participation and punishing non-collaboration.

W:

Kyle S. Blair 2024

Leave Point: The place where a moderator will end the exchange without an understanding.

Discussion terms and procedures can shift, so it's fundamental to really get to know these ideas to explore the exchange cycle actually. Understanding these terms will enable you to impart all the more obviously and settle on informed choices during exchanges One good turn deserves another: A discussion procedure where one party answers in kind to the moves of the other party, compensating participation and punishing non-collaboration.

W:

Leave Point: The place where a moderator will end the exchange without an understanding.

Discussion terms and procedures can shift, so it's fundamental to really get to know these ideas to explore the exchange cycle actually. Understanding these terms will enable you to impart all the more obviously and settle on informed choices during exchanges